ROMY GRIECO

LUCCA
town of art

éditions **ITALCARDS** bologna - italy

Exclusive distribution
RENZO SANTORI - LUCCA
Via Busdraghi, 37 - Telephon 0583/41333

1

History

Lucca's origin dates back to the times of Ligurians, Etruscans and Romans, even though all the findings bear witness to the existence of human settlements since the Paleolithic period. The Celt-Ligurians defined the area where the town now lies with the term «Luk», that is marshland. According to historians, the name dates back to that epoch, but only in the third century b.C., under the Romans, did Lucca start to acquire some relevance. At that time it was a Roman stronghold and, one century later, in 180 b.C., it became a Latin colony. In 89 b.C. it was transformed into a Roman Municipium. Caesar, Crassus and Pompeius met here in Lucca, an event which had a tremendous impact on history.

The town reached its splendour during the first two centuries A.D., of which remarkable traces are still evident, such as the walls, the amphitheatre, etc.

The development of the town was greatly furthered by its strategic location. It is the point of intersection of many ancient roads (Clodia, Aurelia, Cassia) and the Goths and the Longobards made it the capital of Etruria. After the Longobards' conversion to Catholicism, it became a Diocese divided into several parishes. This was the beginning of a second period of political and economic splendour.

A further growth of its prestige was recorded at the time of the first Crusade, in which many people from Lucca took part. After becoming a Commune, in the 13th century its fame spread outside the borders. A flourishing trade started, not only with Europe, but also with Asia. The silk was the most renowned article. In the same period the centre of the town was enriched with architectural works of art, the second circle of walls, many churches and so on. The houses too were embellished and started to acquire a tower-like shape, often surmounted by a green spot, a holm oak planted on the top.

At the same time, however, domestic strifes began to torment the town: the feudal aristocracy on the one side and the trading bourgeoisie on the other, that is Ghibellines and Guelphs. After the triumph of the latter, the struggle went on between Black and White Guelphs. The Black finally prevailed and forced the Antelminelli family to leave the town. Lucca, however, experienced one of its moments of splendour under the rule of one of the most industrious members of this family, Castruccio Castracani. This great «condottiero» managed to extend the town's rule over most of Tuscany. After his death, domestic struggles were resumed, and as a result Lucca fell under the control of Pisa.

Paolo Guinigi ruled Lucca from 1400 to 1430 and encouraged its artistic development, as witnessed by Palazzo Guinigi, Villa Guinigi and the sarcophagus by Jacopo della Quercia which contains the mortal remains of his young wife, Ilaria del Carretto. After his destitution, caused by the aristocrats supporting Francesco Sforza, the Republic of Lucca went through a critical period and Florence established its predominance of that area.

Life in town was deeply shaken, and greater attention was paid to defence problems (by building a new circle of walls), which meant also a shift from trade to agriculture. In this period (16th century) many wonderful villas were built in the country surrounding the town. Most of them are still visible today.

2

1. Panther and coat of arms of the town on the façade of Porta S. Maria; 2. Low relief at the bottom of the Stellario column representing Lucca in the 17th c.; 3. Aerial view; 4. Piazzale San Donato: ancient gate standing back from the present perimeter of the city walls; 5. Porta dei SS. Gervasio e Protasio (13th c.).

5

3

The life of the Republic of Lucca went on without many big changes until the end of the 18th century, when it became part of Napoleon's empire. Lucca was then transformed into a principality ruled by Elisa Baciocchi, sister of the Emperor, until 1814. Three years later it fell under the rule of Parma Bourbons. In 1847 the town joined Tuscany and they became part of the Kingdom of Italy.

1. Keeps of Porta SS. Gervasio e Protasio and houses of Via dei Fossi. In the background, cathedral's campanile; 2. Panorama showing the Tower of Hours (Torre delle Ore), campanile of San Cristoforo and campanile of San Frediano; 3. Section of the medieval city walls contained in the 16th c. wall.

4

The Walls

Italy has a great deal of walled towns, but only few of them have as many as four circles of walls still so largely preserved.

The first one is Roman. It had a quadrangular shape and was probably 8-9 metres high. Today it would run along the following roads: via della Rosa, via dell'Angelo Custode, via Mordini, via degli Asili, via San Giorgio, via Galli Tassi, via San Domenico, via della Cittadella and Corso Garibaldi. It was built in large blocks of limestone, and obviously these walls are not as well preserved as the others. A stretch can still be seen inside the church of Santa Maria della Rosa. The circle had four gates. The northern one, later called San Frediano, led to the Clodia and Cassia roads in the direction of Parma. The eastern one, San Gervasio, led to Florence and Rome; the southern one, St. Peter, led to Pisa; the western one, San Donato, led to Luni.

The second circle of walls dates back to the Middle Ages. It was actually built in the 12th and 13th centuries. Since the town had expanded, it was necessary to protect the new north-eastern districts (San Frediano, San Pietro Somaldi, Santa Maria Forisportam).

The circle was made of squared stones, and had four gates, two of which are still visible: the **Borghi** and the **Santi Gervasio e Protasio**. All four gates had drawbridges and two side-towers. Within this circle of walls a further defence structure was built on initiative of Castruccio Castracani, and on a Giotto plan. This structure, the «Augusta», surrounded one fourth of the town's area limited by two sides of the walls.

The third circle dates back to the 15th century. Some keeps surrounded another area in the north-east. In the south and in the west they confined themselves to building new round-shaped keeps along the old fortifications.

The fourth circle impresses the tourist with its imposingness. It took more than one century to build it,

1. Porta San Pietro (16th c.); 2. Porta San Donato (17th c.); 3. Enchanting night view.

7

which is quite understandable when one thinks of the incredible length of this marvellous «belt»: 4,200 metres.

It was not simply long, but it also had eleven ramparts, twelve curtains, with long rows of trees, and an external ditch with embankements and «demilunes». A huge work of defence, which also private citizens contributed to with dozens of stone cartloads.

The artillery was located in the rampart: 126 cannons which remained there until 1799, when the Austrians removed them. They served as defensive bulwarks, powder magazines, shelters and victuals areas. Underground you could find ammunitions and whatever could be needed to resist a prolonged attack.

Initially, three gates were built: **San Donato, San Pietro** and **Santa Maria**. Napoleon's sister ordered the opening of the fourth gate, **Elisa Gate**, in 1804, in the eastern side. Two further gates were open in more recent times.

What is really peculiar is that actually this majestic and imposing fortification never served as a defence system against the enemies. It was, however, essential in 1812 when a flood could have swept off the whole town which was literally saved by the walls. The river Serchio overflowed its banks and flooded the surrounding countryside, but Lucca remained intact. Even more peculiar is the fact that when Elisa Bonaparte, after receiving news of the flood, tried to enter the town, she was forced to use a crane which lifted her above the walls.

The present appearance of the walls is very attractive: parks, gardens, an unforgettable promenade render the walls absolutely unparalleled.

1. Underground passages of the S. Paolino bastion; 2. Autumn view; 3. The walls under the snow; 4. Sunset on Porta S. Donato; 5. Bastion of Liberty.

1

2

3

PIAZZA DEL GIGLIO

If you are at St. Peter's Gate, corso Garibaldi should be reached through Via San Girolamo, which starts from Via Carrara, and crossed, thus arriving at the **Teatro del Giglio**. This neoclassical building, designed by Lazzarini, stands in a square which bears the same name. In the latter there are a precious monument representing Giuseppe Garibaldi and two beautiful palaces: **Paoli** (which is now a hotel) and **Arnolfini**.

1. Piazzale di Porta San Pietro and oratory of Madonnina; 2. Piazza del Giglio with Theatre; 3. Theatre del Giglio; 4. Interior of the theatre.

PALAZZO DUCALE

On the left of Piazza del Giglio there is Piazza Napoleone also Piazza Grande, which hosts the marvellous **Palazzo Ducale** (or Palazzo della Signoria, as it was defined at the time of the Lucca Republic), or simply called Palazzo Pubblico, which is now the seat of the provincial government. This building has a very eventful past. It rises on part of the area occupied by the Augusta Fortress (mentioned in the chapter dealing with the walls), commissioned by Castruccio Castracani in 1322. When he died, the fortress was occupied by the foreign rulers, which led the inhabitants of Lucca to see it as the symbol of slavery. It was then furiously destroyed by the people. Only the Palazzo della Signoria was saved, and it became the new seat of the Council of the Elders, replacing the former one, located in Piazza San Michele. It was also the residence of the Gonfalonier and the place where the Higher Council held its meetings. Furthermore, it was the seat of the arsenal (called «la Tersenaia»), the Ministry of Finance of that time (the «Offizio sopra l'entrata»), the Gabella Maggiore (the Customs Office through which the state obtained most of its revenue) and the Secret Archive (the «Tarpea»).

Let us examine the complex history of the palace. In the mid-15th century there were three different buildings in the southern part. In August 1567 a lightning caused a terrible explosion in the powder magazine of the palace tower, which resulted in serious damages to the entire building. The palace was not restored, and a new seat for the Lucca government was built. Bartolomeo Ammannati, the architect entrusted with the task of drawing up the project, prepared also a wooden model which clearly represented his harmonious plan.

The project and the model were the object of a long debate, but they were finally approved, even though the loftyness of the building probably appeared excessive for a town which was not the seat of an important political life.

The construction work then began under the supervision of Bartolomeo Ammannati. The parts of the building which are still existing are the left end side of the façade, the northern wing facing the Cortile degli Svizzeri (Swiss Guard's Yard), and the loggia, which leads to the main gate. The loggia has three arches with windows between them. It is decorated and embellished with a marvellous coffered ceiling and a cotto floor. The gate and the porch pillars on the northern and eastern sides of the Cortile degli Svizzeri are rustic. The second yard, now called Carrara, was also created by Ammannati. The gate entrance hall was probably supposed to be the ground floor of the palace tower, which in fact was not built, owing to financial problems. This was not the only work that failed to be carried out. Since it was necessary to fortify the town, Ammannati was dismissed and the building was completed.

The work was undertaken again only at the beginning of the 18th century, under the direction of Juvara, who submitted two plans at twenty years' distance. The first one, which probably was exceedingly ambitious and costly, was rejected, whereas the second one was adopted and the works soon began. The façade was thus completed, the northern wing with the monumental entrance was built, and the second yard built by Ammannati which had been largely damaged, was restored.

Yet, it was fated that Juvara would not complete the work either, and the palace remained without its western side.

1

The third stage of works coincided with the presence of Elisa Bonaparte (when many buildings were pulled down in order to create the square which was given her brother's name) and Marie Louise Bourbon, who entrusted the architect Lorenzo Nottolini with the task of carrying out the works. The existing structures were modified with the aim of creating a connection between the two yards, called «il Passaggio delle Carrozze» (the Carriage Passaggeway). The 16th-century grand staircase was also demolished and replaced by the Royal Staircase leading to the statue gallery. The first floor too was modified and divided in three parts. The first one, used for official events, included a lobby, meeting rooms and the King's private office, and the other two had the King's and Queen's apartments. Of course, the decorative works (frescoes, stuccoes, bas-reliefs) as well as the furniture were very sumptuous.

All these marvellous works, however, no longer exist, since, when Lucca and whole of Tuscany were annexed to the Kingdom of Italy, the palace became a property of the Royal family and all the things it contained ended up in their various residences scattered throughout Italy.

In Lucca, therefore, it will be possible to enjoy the sight of all the elements which could not be moved: the splendid Royal Staircase, the statue gallery, the loggia, the Swiss Guards' room, and a few other.

After visiting this marvellous palace, the sightseeing tour may start again from the Swiss Guards' Yard to reach San Romano church, consecrated in 1821.

1. Ducal Palace; 2. Detail of the façade showing the entrance portal; 3. Courtyard degli Svizzeri; 4. Main courtyard with the statue of the Luccan jurist Francesco Carrara; 5. Statues' gallery.

PALAZZO BERNARDINI

It was built in the 16th century by Nicolao Civitali, and it has all the typical features of the Lucca architecture of those time. The façade, which was enlarged some time after being built, includes the larger portal and the street benches. The original two-light windows of the first floor were then modified. The one on the portal righ-hand side includes what is known as the «Miracle Stone», that is a jamb which gradually bent, as if it had made of wood instead of stone. According to the legend, the jamb moved away from its original position since that had previously been the seat of a holy image, taken away when the palace was modified. Other interesting buildings to be seen in the square are the **Oratory of St. Benedict in Gottella** and **Palazzo Balbani**, built in the 16th century in front of Palazzo Bernardini.

PALAZZO CENAMI

Walking down Via Cenami from Piazza San Giusto you will reach Palazzo Cenami, built in the 16th century. The two façades, which join each other forming an acute angle, have some features which are rather unusual in Lucca, since at their base there are street benches and a rather uncommon stone moulding. The courtyard with a rectangular arcade is worth noting.

ST. ROMANO'S CHURCH

The façade, which was left unfinished, has a beautiful portal. Inside the church, on the side of the apse, there are five chapels which, as is the case of the apse itself, were built with the material obtained from the demolition of the Augusta Fortress nearby. The works of art it contains include a San Vincenzo Ferreri painting of the 15th century, a Sante Pagnini statue, the «St. Stanislao's miracle», paintings by Lombardi and, in the first chapel, an image of St. Romano and his sarcophagus with a valuable bas-relief. Other interesting works are the monument representing the Portico bishops, a «Circumcision» by Manetti, a St. Hyacinth by Passignano ad a Crucifix and St. Thomas by Vanni. The bell-tower is on the northern side and one may reach the Sacristy through the cloister which, on its right-hand side, displays many tombstones coming from gentilitial graves. Among these tombstones, which date back to the 14th and 15th centuries and come from the church's floor, there are those of Capoana Donoratico, the wife of Count Ugolino (the famous character of Dante Alighieri's Divine Comedy) and seven Teutonic knights who were constables at the Augusta Fortress.

Once this part of the tour is over, it is advisable to go out in Via Burlamacchi, cross Via Vittorio Emanuele and reach Piazza Sant'Alessandro to visit its church.

ST. JOHN'S CHURCH

From Piazza Bernardini, one may walk down Via del Gallo, cross Via del Battistero, where antique dealers can be found, and finally reach the extremely suggestive Piazza San Giovanni. The church is dedicated to St. John and St. Reparata, and it was the seat of the first Lucca cathedral until the 8th century. Recent studies gave evidence that the pillars base and the original crypt date back up the 5th or 6th centuries. Apparently it was rebuilt in the 12th. Though this is not supported by concrete evidence, a temple was probably present in this site in Roman times. In fact, a mosaic was found three metres below the present floor.

Another suggestive element is the romanesque portal with a carved architrave. Inside this church too there are three naves, with columns which probably came from other previous constructions. From the left of the transept one can reach the baptistry dating back to the 14th century. The building is square-shaped and it has a very large ogival dome built at the end of the 14th century. Inside the church there is an image portraying the Virgin Mary with Angels and several other interesting works, which we hope may be visited, since the restoration works began as long as 20 years ago.

When one leaves the church, one finds himself surrounded by an extremely harmonious «ensemble» of artistic works. Before visiting the Cathedral, whose

1. Palazzo Bernardini (1512) by Nicolao Civitali; 2. Entrance portal; 3. Palazzo Cenami (1530) by Civitali; 4. Church of San Romano; 5. Church of San Giovanni; 6. Lunette and lintel of the portal. On the lintel are carved the Madonna between two angels and Saints, dating back to 1187.

15

works of art will absorb so much of your time, it is advisable to take a look at **Piazza Antelminelli** and **Piazza San Marino** (with **Palazzo Micheletti**, probably designed by Ammannati), the seat of the **Opera del Duomo**, the **Oratorio della Maddalena** etcetera. A round-shaped fountain by Lorenzo Nottolini, built in 1832, stands in Piazza Antelminelli. You may also be interested in noting the polychrome materials used for the façade of the Opera del Duomo. Palazzo Micheletti was built in the second half of the 16th century by Giovanni Battista Bernardi, bishop of Ajaccio, who was native from Lucca. The project is attributed to Ammannati. The high wall with balustrades surrounding the garden is particularly valuable. Leaning on St. John's church, it links the two squares.

ST. ALEXANDER'S CHURCH

St. Alexander's church, a Romanesque building erected in the 11th century by order of bishop Anselmo, who then became Pope Alexander II, is one of the few examples of the architecture of that period which may be seen in Lucca. Its façade is white and grey and without ornaments, and its only decorating elements are the statue of the saint sitting on the throne and four small windows. The front gate is very beautiful and so is the one on the church's side, surmounted by a 15th century shrine. The apse is decorated with 13th-century small arches. This very simple and plain architectural elements has colonnades which, in ancient times, surrounded the choir. Many columns and some capitals come from Roman buildings.

2

SAN GIUSTO'S CHURCH

Leaving the church and walking back along Via Vittorio Emanuele, you will reach Piazza San Giusto, where you may visit the church with a nice Romanesque façade, unfortunately disfigured by an ugly block of flats recently built on the foundations of ancient buildings.

The church, built in the 12th and 13th centuries, has a main portal with a large carved architrave. Inside, there are three naves with cotto pillars.

1

ST. CHRISTOPHER'S CHURCH

After visiting Palazzo Cenami, you cannot miss St. Christopher's church. It was built in the 12th and 13th centuries. Inside, it is divided into three naves by two lines of rectangular-section pillar and four columns on which a larger arch stands. There is an interesting 13th-century fresco portraying the Virgin Mary. Underneath there is a memorial slab dedicated to two dead children, the sons of Matteo Civitali. The latter too is buried inside the church.

St. Christopher's church played an important role in the history of the town, since in the 13th century it was the seat of the «Merchants' University». On both sides of the main portal one can still see the two iron bars introduced by the Consuls as the measure for the combs of Lucca's looms. In the 15th century the church had many decorations which were gradually removed in the course of time.

1. Church of Sant'Alessandro; 2. Niche of the lateral portal (15th c.); 3. Church of San Giusto; 4. Decoration of the main portal; 5. Church of San Cristoforo; 6. Piazza Antelminelli. On the next pages: Panorama of the campanile of San Martino, on the right loggias of the third storey of the façade.

17

1. Palazzo Micheletti; 2. Walls of Palazzo Micheletti with the cupola and the campanile of S. Giovanni (baptistry); 3. House of the Cathedral's treasure.

THE CATHEDRAL

You have now come to the most interesting visit of your tour, or perhaps just one of them, since Lucca is full of these masterpieces. We suggest, therefore, that you devote much time to the visit of the Cathedral.

The Cathedral, or St. Martin's church, was first built in the 6th century by order of St. Frediano — this is what the tradition says, at least. Not very much, however, remains of that period, since in the 11th century the bishop Anselmo da Baggio, who later became Pope Alexander II, had it completely rebuilt and consecrated it in the presence of Matilde di Canossa in 1070. But this was not all. In fact, in the following century further restoration was initiated and completed only two centuries later.

Most probably, the oldest part of the whole building is the façade which was leaned against the pre-existing one built in the 11th century. The yard is particularly imposing with its three arcades, supported by composite pillars, and its three elegant small loggias, by Guidetto, decorated in white and green and dating back to the beginning of the 14th century. The

three portals surmounted by lunettes host a Deposition by Pisano and, in the architrave, the Annunciation, Nativity and Adoration by the same artist, on the left; an Ascension and, in the architrave, the Virgin Mary and the Apostles in the centre; the «Martyrdom of St. Regolo» and, in the architrave, the «Disputation of St. Regolo» on the right. On the sides of the central portal there are marble slubs representing the twelve months and the «Stories of St. Martin».

Strangely enough, the right portal is much narrower than the other two. Probably, its width had to be limited because of the pre-existing bell-tower. An expert eye will then realize that the façade was left unfinished. It lacks the final row of small loggias and the tympanum. If it had been completed, it would have been larger in size, like St. Michael church, which was built by the same team of workers.

Before going into the church, have a look at the semi-pillar on the right, close to the bell-tower, with the Labyrinth, the symbolic figure which in those times was placed at the entrance of many churches.

Once you are in, you can start your treasure-hunt. On the right-hand side you have the 14th-century marble group representing St. Martin and the poor man, which was originally on the façade, the author of which is probably a Lombard master. The internal subdivision into three naves is emphasized by the beautiful floor made of green-striped white marble squares embellished with inlaid work. The beautiful holy water stoups near the first two pillars were designed by Matteo Civitali at the end of the 15th century.

Over the third altar on the right there is a «Last Supper» by Tintoretto and others, and canvasses by Passignano, Zuccari and Ridolfi. The altar, like all the others on the same side, is by Piccardi (16th century). At the end of this side there is the door to the Sacristy which was completed at the beginning of the 15th century. The lovely capitals of the semi-pillars have been attributed to Jacopo della Quercia. The «Cantoria» near the door and the pulpit in front of it are by Matteo Civitali. The Sacristy, once named after St. Apollinare, contains a Virgin sitting on the throne with Child by Ghirlandaio, an Annunciation by Grazia, a God the Father by Marti and a detached fresco attributed to Filippino Lippi.

The St. Agnello altar deserves special attention. While the bas-relief portraying the saint is by Pardini, the panel of the Virgin of the throne with four Saints is by Ghirlandaio. The latter's pupil, Bartolomeo di Giovanni, is probably the author of the decorations in the predella. The lunette with the dead Christ supported by Niccodemus is attributed to Filippino Lippi. On the left-hand side of the altar you have a triptych with gold background by the 14th-century Lucca school, and on the right-hand side you have a 15th-century Florence school panel portraying the Virgin with Angels and Saints. On the northern wall there is an Annunciation by Leonardo Grazia, of the first half of the 15th century.

From the Sacristy you can move on to the right transept with the Holy Sacrament chapel, by Vincenzo

Civitali, and the sepulchral monuments to Domenico Bertini and Pietro da Noceto by the same author. He is also responsible for the two adoring angels which probably belong to another altar which later disappeared.

The head of the right nave hosts the St. Agnello altar. The precinct of the choir in the presbytery is attributed to the Civitali school. The High Altar is by

1. Aerial view of Piazza San Martino; 2. Church of San Martino; 3. Apsidal wall of the Cathedral and Bishop's Palace.

23

Vambrè, the choir by Marti. In the vault you can admire the glazed windows by Pandolfo and the Trinity by Gherardi.

In the head of the left nave there is the Liberty Altar, with one of the most renowned works in the cathedral: the «Resurrection of Christ» by Giambologna, with St. Paolino and St. Peter on its sides. The beautiful view of Lucca depicted in the predella dates back to the 16th century and reminds us of the fact that the altar was built to thank God for the regained freedom. Not too far, there is a statue of St. John the Evangelist by Jacopo della Quercia, which was once placed in the northern side of the church. In the tran-

San Martino. 1. Central portal: lunette showing Christ rising to Heaven between two angels; on the lintel, the Apostles and Mary attending the Ascension; 2-3. Story of Saint Martin and the months; 4. The labyrinth carved on a half pilar decorating the campanile at the porch entrance to the narthex; 5. Decorative panel; 6. Central nave; 7. Saint Martin on horseback and the Poor, on the reverse side of the façade; 8. Cantoria of the organ.

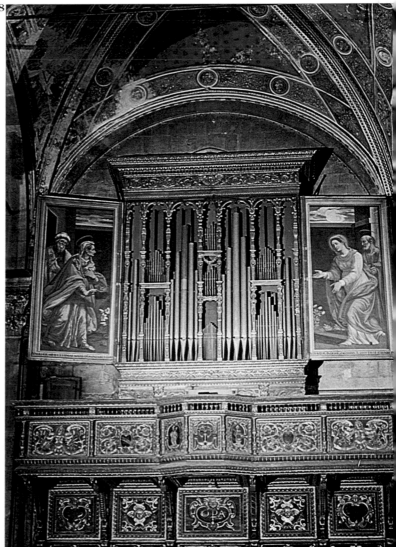

sept, then, you have the Chapel of the Shrine which hosts an altar-piece by Fra' Bartolomeo della Porta portraying the Virgin with Child and saints surrounded by two angels, and the monument to the Guidiccioni bishops. The most remarkable work of art, however, is probably the sarcophagus of Ilaria del Carretto by Jacopo della Quercia, one of the most famous monuments in Luca. Ilaria was Paolo Guinigi's second wife, who died in 1405. The sepulchral monument celebrates her dignified and serene beauty and impresses all the visitors. The sarcophagus was built by Jacopo della Quercia two or three years after the gentlewoman's death. The wonderful puttoes around the sarcophagus and the Guinigi-del Carretto coat-of-arms sculptured on one side are really worth noting.

Halfway through the left nave, there is another interesting work of art. The small temple of the «Volto Santo» designed by Matteo Civitali. It has an octagonal shape and is surmounted by a small dome divided in eight gores. Inside, there is a famous and largely venerated Crucifix which, according to the legend, was carved from a cedar of Lebanon by Niccodemus. The Christ was hidden for a long time in the period of persecutions, and was one day placed in a boat and entrusted to the sea. The boat, according to the legend, sailed through the Mediterranean Sea and was guided by the angels to the shore of Luni. Then the holy image was put on a cart drawn by wild oxen which meakly took it to Lucca. From that period on, the Crucifix has always been object of veneration, making many miracles marking the history of the town. This is the rea-

1

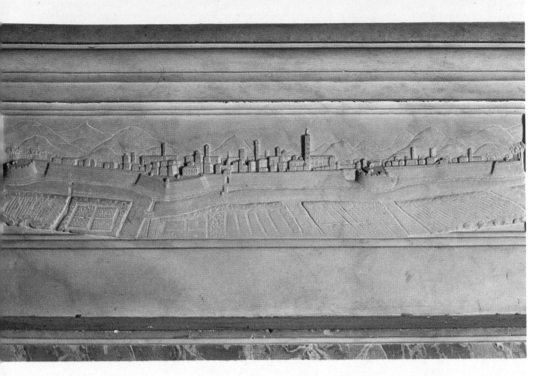

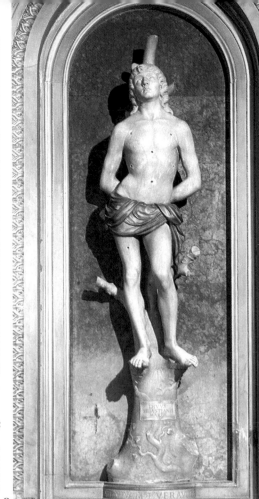

San Martino. 1. Third altar on the right: Last Supper by Tintoretto, dating back to 1590-91, painted specifically for this altar; 2. Socle of the altar of liberty showing Lucca in the 16th c. and the construction of the new city wall (1577). Low relief by John of Bologna; 3. Chapel of the Holy Face: S. Sebastiano (1484) di Matteo Ciritali; 4. Chapel of the Sacrament. Worshipping angel (1473-77), Matteo Civitali; 5. Chapel of the Sanctuary. Virgin and Infant Jesus on the throne between Saint Stephen and Saint John the Baptist (1509 by Frà Bartolomeo della Porta).

2

4 5

3

1

2

San Martino - Sacristy. 1. Altar retable representing Virgin and Infant on the throne between Saint Peter, Saint Clement, Saint Sebastian and Saint Paul, by Domenico Ghirlandaio (1449-1494). Socle of the altar retable representing the lives of saints executed in Ghirlandaio's workshop (late 15th c., beginning of the 16th c.); 2. Saint Matthew, Saint Peter led by the angel from his prison; 3. Saint Clement thrown into the sea on Trajan's orders; 4. Pietà; 5. Martyrdom of Saint Sebastian; 6. Saint Paul's conversion, Saint Laurence.

29

1

son why many coins of the period bear the holy image. Since then, each year, in September, when, according to the legend, the Christ arrived in Lucca, the whole town solemnly celebrates this event and the Crucifix is adorned with precious robes.

Those who are more interested in history of art can, however, find this second version more reliable. The Crucifix was probably made by a Lombard master, under Pope Alexander, in the framework of restoration works of the temple which in those times hosted another Crucifix which no longer exists. The holy image is made of polychrome wood, darkened by the passing of centuries and the smoke of candles. The fame of the Crucifix has crossed Lucca's border, arriving even in France (probably brought here by ancient minstrels) where they venerate «Saint Vaudeluc», that is nothing else but «Saint Vault de Lucques».

In front of the chapel, on the church's wall, there is a fresco by Cosimo Rosselli, illustrating the various phases of the legend, while the altar hosts a «Presen-

2

1. Sarcophagus of Ilaria del Carretto, second wife of Paolo Guinigi, executed by Jacopo della Quercia in 1405, and details.

30

tation of Our Lady in the Temple» by Bronzino (1508)

To end this visit you are advised to take a look at the house of the «Opera del Duomo» where numerous treasures are hosted, which unfortunately are not visible. Among them there is a wonderfully chiselled silver Crucifix which is exhibited in St. Martin's on the day of the procession.

Walking along the northern side of the church, you come to Piazza Arrigoni with the Archbishops' Palace and the Archive with the beautiful portal by Jacopo della Quercia's pupils.

This was the last visit of the second itinerary. Here again we must say that while visiting a church or admiring the façade of an ancient palace, you could also make a few deviations in some of the Lucca's lanes (chiassi) or in the garden of a house, to take less famous, but equally suggestive, views.

San Martino. 1. «Tempietto» of the Volto Santo, executed in 1482 by Matteo Civitali; built in white Carrara marmor with red porphyry sheets, of octogonal shape with a composite column surmounted by entablature at each corner and topped by a cupola finishing with a lantern figuring Bertini's motto: «So that I may live in real life»; 2. Medieval wooden carving; 3. Statue of the Santo Volto used during the feast of the Saint Cross; 4. Detail of the medieval wooden carving.

1

2   3

VILLA GUINIGI

The palace has an elongated shape and two façades. It was built in the first decades of the 15th century by Paolo Guinigi, Lord of Lucca. The enterprise cost a huge amount of money: 76,00 guilds. The palace was inaugurated on August 7th, 1420, on the occasion of the second marriage of Guinigi. He lost the property of the palace only 40 years later, when he was defeated and his building was confiscated and much of its content was lost. The garden was really sumptuous, but only part of it is still existing. The rest was devoured by the town development. However, it still contains the statue of Charles III, some garden statues, blocks of tuff from the old wall and mosaics.

The façade of Villa Guinigi is characterized by a set of three-light windows and a central double porch with eight arches (on the back there are only seven of them).

The finds kept inside are particularly interesting. In the northern loggia, for instance, there are some capitals coming from the façade of St. Michael's church and in the adjacent rooms Roman and Etruscan fragments are displayed; in particular there are sepulchral

San Martino. 1. Presentation of Mary at the temple (1598), by Alessandro Allori known as il Bronzino; 2. View of Villa Guinigi now National Museum.

fittings of several Etruscan and Ligurian tombs. In the southern loggia there are bronze bells and two tombstones: one of Balduccio Parghia degli Antelminelli by Jacopo della Quercia and one of Caterina degli Antelminelli, by the school of the same artist. The adjacent rooms contain Romanesque, Gothic and Renaissance sculptures, 8th-13th century statues, taken here from churches which have disappeared or have been transformed, a «Virgin with Child» in stained gilded marble attributed to Civitali, once placed in the Loggia dei Mercanti (Merchants' Loggia), which unfortunately went lost. You can also admire a marble high-relief, «Samson Fighting Against the Lion», by a Master from Lucca, some detached frescoes, Baccio da Montelupo's tombstone, tabernacles, high-reliefs, several 17th-19th century sculptures and the famous «misure Lucchesi» (Lucca measures), that is weight and measuring instruments of the Republic of Lucca.

You can then climb the stairs, along which many coats-of-arms are displayed, and reach the vestibule, which hosts the coats-of-arms of the Guinigi Orsetti family and numerous wooden works of the Lucca art: in particular, a two-door wardrobe, made of carved wood by Alberto and Arduino da Baiso and probably belonging to Paolo Guinigi's library; four stalls of the choir of the cathedral inlaid by Leonardo Marti; a bust

by Civitali representing St. Martin; the doors of the wardrobe of the sacristy of St. Martin's church by Cristoforo Canozzi da Lendinara, who was a friend of Piero della Francesca's and, like him, was able to illustrate towns and landscapes with an incredible mastery of perspective; and other works among which we shall mention a 16th-century medallion with Paolo Guinigi's profile, various armchairs and a marvellous Sienese painting, entitled «Visitation», uncertainly ascribable to Giacomo Pacchiarotti or to Francesco di Giorgi.

The adjacent room contains three crucifixes: the first one is on a 12th-century panel and is one of the oldest works of art from Lucca; the second one, by Berlinghiero, dates back to the beginning of the 13th century; the third one was made at the end of the same century by Deodato Orlandi, an artist from Lucca. In the same room there are also a predella by Ugolino di Neri and two small panels by Ugolino Lorenzetti, originally part of a polyptych which was lost, and representing the Virgin and St. John the Evangelist.

In room 12 you can admire a Virgin with Child of Flemish school, a triptych by Angelo Puccinelli, a Lucca artist of the 14th century, a tabernacle with three niches by Priamo della Quercia, Jacopo's brother, which the Lucca people call «dei pimpinnacoli», for the kind of decoration it has.

Room 13 too is very rich. Here you can see two panels, attributed to two 15th-century painters from Lucca, Michele Ciampianti and Antonio Corsi. The two panels represent the Immaculate Conception and the Virgin's Coronation. Other works contained in the room are: a 10th-century German-school triptych attributed to Martin Heemskerk; paintings by Lorenzo di Pietro, called «il Vecchietto» (in particular, the «Dormitio Virginis» which was completed by one of his pupils); three works by the Master of «Tondo» Lathrop, a 16th-century Lucca painter; many paintings of the Botticelli school, by Filippino Lippi, Neroccio di Bartolomeo and others, together with a nice bench by Salimbene Magni.

In room 14 there is another bench by Zacchia da Vezzano, one of the most important Lucca painters of the 16th century, two large canvasses by Fra' Bartolomeo (The Eternal appears to Mary Magdalene and St. Caterina from Siena and the Virgin of the Mercy) and a Virgin in glory with saints by Amigo Aspertini.

In the corridor you will be able to admire two inlaid wooden doors, an Adoration of the Sheperds by Zacchia da Vezzano and the Adoration by Lorenzo Zacchia, a Nativity of Our Lady, by Riccio, a Visitation by Massei, a Visitation by Paolo Guidotti, a Cumaean

National Museum. 1. Virgin and Infant. Painted and gilted marmor low relief by Matteo Civitali; 2. Pluteus: Samson fighting against the lion. High relief in marmor and part of the background in marquetry. Luccan master of the second half of the 12th c.; 3. Exhibition room of the museum: on the right, Eternal Father and Saints (1509) by Frà Bartolomeo; 4. View of the city. Wooden marquetry by Cristoforo Canozzi da Lendinara (15th c.); 5. The Bishop Saint Martin. Wooden marquetry by Cristoforo Canozzi da Lendinara (15th c.).

3

4 5

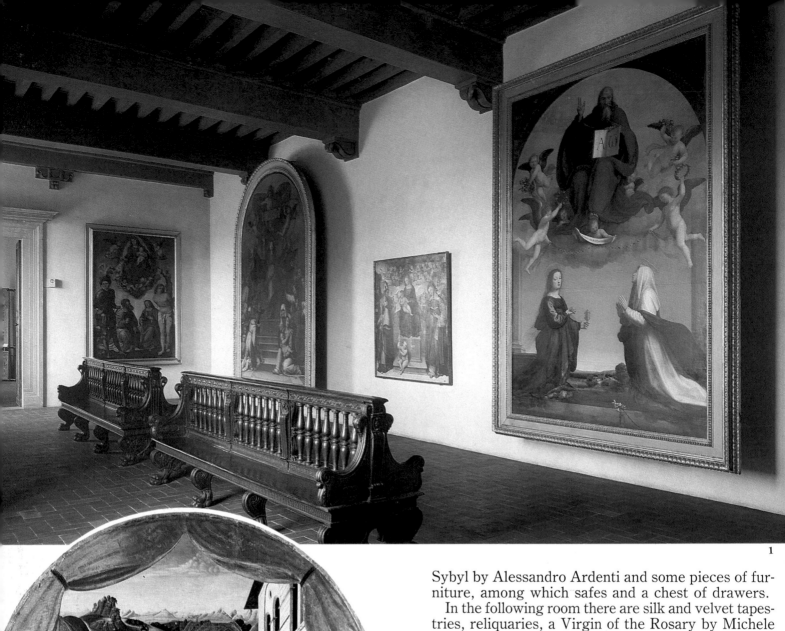

Sybyl by Alessandro Ardenti and some pieces of furniture, among which safes and a chest of drawers.

In the following room there are silk and velvet tapestries, reliquaries, a Virgin of the Rosary by Michele di Ridolfo, a «St. Peter heals the cripple» by Passignano. Room 17 contains further tapestries, crucifixes, Longobard plates, chasubles, thuribles and three canvasses by Vasari. In room 18 it is worthwhile looking at a «Martyrdom of San Ponziano», a «Martyrdom of St. Bartholomew», a «Nativity of St. John the Baptist» by Paolini, a Pietà attributed to Matteo Civitali and a Deposition by Lomi. The 17th-century fireplace is also worth seeing.

The last two rooms host a Presentation of the Wirgin Mary in the Temple and an Adoration of the Kings by Lombardi, a Trinity by Brugieri, an image of San Vincenzo Ferreri by Diecimino, a Prie-Dieu, three works by Pompeo Batoni (the Arch-bishop Giovan Domenico Mansi, a Martyrdom of St. Bartholomew and the Ecstasy of St. Catherine) and the «Cry of Ulysses» by Nocchi).

National Museum. 1. View of an exhibition room; 2. Visitation (late 15th c.), attributed either to Giacomo Pacchiarotti or Francesco di Giorgio; 3. Crucifix. Table tempera (13th c.) by Berlinghieri.

38

1

2

3

4

National Museum. 1. Virgin and Infant (14th c.) by Ugolino Lorenzetti; 2. Virgin and Infant and Saint Sebastian and Saint Rocco (16th c.) by Zacchia il Vecchio; 3. Virgin and Infant between Saint Stephen and Saint Jerome (11th c.). «Maestro del tondo Lathrop»; 4. Portrait of the Archbishop Giovan Domenico Mansi (18th c.); 5. Ecstasy of Saint Catherine (1773) by Pompeo Batoni.

ST. FRANCIS' CHURCH

The church, reconstructed in the 14th century, has two arks on the façade dating back to the 13th and 14th centuries. The façade is in white marble and its upper part has been modified recently. Inside, there is one nave, with a truss-ceiling, a sepulchral monument to Bishop Guidiccioni made by Baccio da Montelupo, a memorial slab dedicated to Castruccio Castracani degli Antelminelli, 15th-century frescoes by Ghirlandaio, Gozzoli, Rosselli, remains of the monument to Nino Visconti, and other frescoes which, unfortunately, are severely damaged.

The choir and lectern of the Cappella Maggiore are by Marchi (15th century). On the left you have a Nativity by Zuccari and the tombs of two Lucca musicians, Boccherini and Geminiani. Along the northern side of the church there are the 13th-century Sacristy and the three cloisters of the convent, with some Medieval tombs. On one of these, the Tignosini tomb, there is a lunette frescoed by Deodato Orlandi.

VIA DEL FOSSO

Further on you will come to Via del Fosso, which owes its name to the canal dividing Lucca in two parts. It is worthwhile stopping for a minute to have a look at this part of Lucca with its small houses. Then, you are advised to cross one of the small bridges and you will enjoy the lovely sight of the **San Gervasio and Protasio Gate**, also called «Portone dell'Annunziata». This is what remains of the circle of Medieval walls, together with the two keeps whose merlons were lost. The actual gate is made of sandstone with stripes of white limestone. The southern keep is linked to the **small church of Santa Maria Annunziata** or «dell'Alba» with a lovely Renaissance portico.

1. Church of San Francesco (14th c.); 2. Column figuring Madonna dello Stellario (1687) by the sculptor G. Lazzoni di Carrara; 3. View of Via dei Fossi. In the foreground detail of a mascaron of the neo-classical fountain; 4. Villa Buonvisi (1566); 5. View of Via dei Fossi. On the right the wall surrounding Villa Buonvisi's park; 6. Chiesetta (small church) di Santa Maria Annunziata also known as Church of the Dawn (14th c.).

5 6

SANTA MARIA FORISPORTAM

Take now Via Santa Croce down to the church of Santa Maria Forisportam, otherwise known as Santa Maria Bianca, wich was originally outside the Roman walls.

Curiously enough, the church seems to have no foundations, because subsequent stratifications over centuries have hidden the basement. It dates back to the 12th century and has a beautyful façade with three finely sculptured portals, with precious architraves, trusses and mouldings. The façade is coated with white marble and has two rows of small loggias. The lunettes of the portals host a «Virgin sitting on the Throne» on the left, a «Coronation of the Virgin» in the centre, both of the 17th century, and a Bishop of the 13th century on the right. The architraves are decorated with a lion, bronze roses and a griffon, respectively.

Inside, there are three Romanesque naves. The central nave was raised with bricks in the 16th century, together with the transept. The High Altar, with the statue of the Assumption, is by Civitali. In the fourth altar on the right you can admire an image of St. Lucy by Guercino. The lovely early-Christian sarcophagus is now used as a baptismal font. On the altar in the right transept there is a 17th-century cyborium. The left transept hosts a monument to Antonio Mazzarosa and panels with the «Dormitio Virginis» and the Assumption by Puccinelli (14th century). The crypt, which originally was as large as the transept, has completely disappeared.

Outside there is a remarkable bell-tower and a Roman column in the centre of the square, which was, until the 18th century, goal of the arrival of the «Palio» run on certain special occasions. In the southern side of the square you can admire **Palazzo Sirti**, by Martinelli, built at the end of the 17th century and, in front, **Palazzo Penitesi**.

PIAZZA SAN PIETRO SOMALDI

The view which can be taken from the square is marvellous, surrounded as it is by 16th-century palaces (**Palazzo Bartolomei, Spada**, etc.).

The church is named after its founder, who had it built in the period of the Longobards and whose name was Sumuald. It was completely rebuilt at the end of the 12th century and further restored until the 16th century. The façade is made of sandstone and striped with white limestone, like many other churches in Lucca. In the upper part there are two rows of small loggias. The beautiful bell-tower is made of sandstone in its lower part, while the top was added when the façade was completed and it was made of red brick with «eyes» and small columns.

The architrave of the central door is worth seeing. It was probably designed at the beginning of the 13th century by Guido Bigarelli. It depicts the keys being given to St. Peter. There are three naves, separated by rectangular pillars. The most interesting works of art are a 16th-century Assumption by Zacchia da Vezzano over the left altar, a panel portraying some saints attributed to Raffaellino del Garbo, an artist working at the turn of the 16th century. Other interesting paintings by Tofanelli, Landucci and Franchi are displayed.

SANTA MARIA DELLA ROSA

Walking down Via della Rosa, on the left of the square, you will get to the church of Santa Maria della Rosa.

It was built at the beginning of the 14th century by the Università dei Mercanti, and then enlarged and dedicated to St. Mary of the Rose. The oldest part of the oratory is on the right hand side, with a portal and two-light windows. In a second phase, four-light windows surrounded by arches were added. The portal of the façade is attributed to Civitali. The three naves inside are separated by beautiful columns and, on the left, there are the ruins of the old 2nd-century Roman walls in big squared blocks. Outside Santa Maria della Rosa we suggest to go up to the near bulwark of San Colombano, before walking down the road and turning left in Via dell'Arcivescovado to approach the **church of Santa Maria dei Servi**.

1. Church of Santa Maria Forisportam (12th c.); 2. Lunette of the central portal figuring the coronation of the Virgin (13th c.) and decorated lintel; 3. Church of San Pietro Somaldi (12th-14th c.); 4. Detail of the façade; 5. Sculpted lintel of the portal representing the handing over of the keys to Saint Peter (attributed to Guido Bigarelli); 6. Church of Santa Maria della Rosa (14th c.).

PALAZZO GUINIGI

Here you are, now, in front of the most important monument of the third itinerary, Palazzo Guinigi. These are, in fact, two palaces, one in front of the other, surmounted by a beautiful, slender tower decorated by the green crowns of holm oaks which in the past embellished almost all the towers.

At the base of the brick-made palaces there are arcades supported by stone pillars. The main palace, the one with the tower, has three-, four- and five-light windows surmonted by little arches. Originally also the other palace had its own tower, and you can still notice its ruins on the right side. Today the palace is owned by the Municipality which has restored it and has consolidated the access to the tower. It is therefore possible today to reach the top and admire the wonderful, impressive panorama of the town lying below.

PIAZZA ANFITEATRO ROMANO

Piazza Anfiteatro is named after the ancient **Roman Amphitheatre** with an ellyptical shape, built between the 1st and the 2nd centuries A.D. Thanks to ancient documents, it is known that it was made of two rows of arches and pillars (probably 54), which supported the 24 steps of the cavea where 10,000 people could sit. The ruin of this imposing theatre started at the times of Barbarian invasions, after which the amphitheatre became a sort of cave for the reconstruc-

1

2

1. Tower and Palazzo Guinigi; 2. Tower Guinigi and Tower of Hours; 3-4. Different views of Piazza dell'Anfiteatro.

46

3

tion of all the buildings in town. Columns, marbles and everything useful was removed, just leaving shapeless ruins which were subsequently covered by further layers (at present, the amphitheatre is three metres below the ground) and used as solid foundation for other constructions. People, in fact, started to build the first modest houses on these ruins keeping the curved shape of the Roman theatre, but giving a somewhat chaotic aspect to the ensemble, which lasted from the Middle Ages until the 19th century. In 1830, Carlo Ludovico, Duke of Lucca, asked the architect Lorenzo Nottolini to rearrange the whole area. Nottolini just decided to level out all the houses built on the amphitheatre at the first floor, leaving them rise as much as possible (three or four floors) without any special concern. He also ordered the demolition of some small buildings within, and the result was the square which can be still admired for its harmony.

On the eastern side there are the few original elements of the amphitheatre with an arch entrance. Three other openings were obtained in the 19th century.

4

The Roman Amphitheatre which is now approximatively three metres under the ground was built outside the city walls in the first or second century. Of elliptical shape it was made on the outside of two superposed rows of 54 arcades on pilar which supported the cavea itself made of 24 tiers. This large building, destroyed during the Barbarian invasions, was used for centuries as a quarry for building materials. The extraordinary square which we now see was designed in 1830 by the architect Lorenzo Nottolini who showed inspired urbanistic intuition: he had the few buildings standing in the arena pulled down and then completed at the ground level the circular row of houses which was interrupted in places without touching the extreme variety of levels. The overall effect is really remarkable.

Aerial view of Piazza Anfiteatro and Basilica San Frediano. On page 51: Tower of Hours.

48

TORRE DELLE ORE

Now, going back through the square and being guided by its silhouette, you can reach the **Torre delle Ore** (Clock Tower), which in the past was called Torre della Lite (Tower of the Quarrel) because it had been the object of many struggles between rival families.

You will therefore walk in the shadow of many medieval buildings and then raise your eyes to look at the only one of the 130 towers existing in Lucca in the Middle Ages which has survived. Many of them collapsed, other were destroyed or lowered at the times of Castruccio Castracani in order to use their stones to build the Augusta fortress. This particular tower has probably survived because it has always had a public clock which the people wanted to preserve.

1. Via Fillungo with Tower of Hours; 2. Via Fillungo. Old Café di Sino where used to meet in the past writers and artists such as Pascoli, Puccini, Ungaretti etc.; 3. Via Fillungo. Old Oreficeria Carli (goldsmith's trade); 4. View of Via Fillungo; 5. View from above with San Frediano's belfry.

ST. FREDIANO'S CHURCH

After visiting this ensemble, take the direction of Piazza degli Scalpellini, where you can have a look at **Palazzo Moriconi**, built in the 14th century and totally restructured in the following century. Then, go on along Via Fillungo (where you can admire **Palazzo Buonvisi**, **Palazzo Guinigi Magrini** and **Palazzo Cenami Menocchi** on the right). You now reach Piazza San Frediano, with the church bearing the same name and, obviously, dedicated to him. Here, in the 6th century the Bishop Frediano built the Basilica Langobardorum dedicated to St. Vincent. The name was modified when Bishop John decided to reconstruct the building placing his predecessor's tomb inside.

The present appearance of the church is the result of various reconstructions, restorations and embellishments. The first intervention was called for by the Prior of the Monastery, Rotone, who had it raised three metres and modified the façade and the apse. The church was consecrated by Pope Eugene III in 1147. Later on, between the 14th and the 15th centuries, the lateral chapels were added to the three original central naves.

The façade is adorned with the wonderful Byzantine mosaic illustrating Christ's Ascension, by a row of small columns and a beautiful portal with a 12th-century architrave.

Inside, on the right, you will see the marvellous Romanesque baptismal font, which was reassembled a few decades ago, after it had been dismantled at the end of the 18th century. It is signed by Master Roberto, and bears on the outer side the story of Moses and figures. On the «lid» of the higher basin there are decorations representing the months and the Apostles. On the nearby wall you can admire a glaced terra-cotta lunette attributed to Andrea della Robbia and illustrating the Annunciation.

On the same side there is a badly preserved fresco by Amico Aspertini, depicting the Virgin with the Child and Saints.

Most probably, the columns of the central nave were taken from the Roman amphitheatre.

The chapels are full of precious works of art. The 17th-century Fatinelli chapel hosts a canvas by Guidotti, the tomb of St. Zita with paintings by Tintore illustrating the miracles of the Saint who lived in the 13th century. One of these miracles is the transformation of bread into flowers which the Saint performed when she was discovered by the master (she worked as a servant in the Fatinelli family), while she was helping the poor by hiding the bread taken from the house in her lap. Being asked what she was jealously concealing, the Saint answered that she carried flowers, and the bread of the poor was transformed into flow-

1. Church of San Frediano (12-13th c.); 2. Mosaique of the façade (13th c.) representing Christ rising to Heaven in a mandorla carried by two angels while the apostles are watching. It has some byzantine features and was executed by Berlinghieri's school.

ers. In order to celebrate the miracle, each year, in April, the square is filled with flowers, while people take the newly bloomed jonquils into the church to have them blessed.

Close to the chapel there is an image of St. Batholomew, probably by della Robbia.

Cenami chapel, also called San Biagio, contains a Deposition by Paolini and wooden statues by Matteo Civitali.

In Micheli chapel you will find an Assumption by Masseo Civitali (not to be confused with Matteo, who was his uncle) and a monument to Lazzaro Papi in the presbitery.

The floor behind the High Altar dates back to 12th century and was taken here from the choir area when the present altar was built, in the 17th century. On the left side of the church, Trentas' chapel hosts a masterpiece by Jacopo della Quercia: an altar frontal in five pieces made in 1422. In the centre there is the Virgin with Child and the four side panels portray St. Ursula, St. Lawrence, St. Jerome and St. Richard. In the

predella there is a Pietà and the miracles and martyrdoms of the Saints portrayed in the panels. A St. Richard sarcophagus is placed under the altar close to the tombs of Lorenzo Trenta and his wife by della Quercia. In front of the altar there is a work by Francia, «Conception of the Virgin», and a statue by Civitali portraying St. Peter.

The Gentilis' chapel, also named after St. Augustine, has a 17th-century tabernacle, many frescoes by Amico Aspertini, a Nativity of Christ, stories of St. Frediano, St. Ambrose baptizing St. Augustine, and the famous Transportation of the Holy Face from Luni to Lucca. According to some historians, some of the faces in the frescoes by Aspertini are the portraits of rich people of that period, including the author.

The Buonvisi chapel hosts the monument to Cardinals Bonviso, Jerome and Francis Buonvisi, a painting by Nocchi depicting St. Anne (on the left), a Nativity of Our Lady (right), and other canvasses by Tofanelli.

The church also contains, in the head of the left nave, a limestone monolyth, probably coming from the amphitheatre, near a sepulchral slab taken from St. Frediano's sarcophagus which has been lost. The 16th-century organ by Domenico di Lorenzo is worth seeing too.

Church of San Frediano. 1. View of the interior; 2. View of the interior with in the foreground a baptismal font (12th c.) Circular basin containing an internal bowl, supported by a pilar and crowned with small columns with capital; 3. Detail of the baptismal front. It is one of the six panels encircling the external basin and representing the Crossing of the Red Sea; 4. Lunette in glazed terracotta picturing the Annunciation, attributed to Andrea della Robbia. 4

3

4

Church of San Frediano. *1. Altar front of the Chapel Trenta executed by Jacopo della Quercia who finished it in 1422. In the middle, Virgin and Infant; on the left: Saint Ursula and Saint Laurence; on the right, Saint Jerome and Saint Richard. On the left-hand sided predella: Saint Catherine of Alexandria, martyrdom of Saint Ursula and of her companions, martyrdom of Saint Laurence, Pietà and two afflicted, Saint Jerome removing the thorn from the lion's foot, curing of the possessed in front of Saint Richard's body, Saint Ursula; 2. Detail of the altar front; 3. Polychrome wooden statue of the Virgin of the Annunciation by Matteo Civitali (15th c.); 4. Chaste body of the virgin Saint Zita (1218-1278).*

2

1

2

3

The Sacristy hosts many valuable sacred items: a 12th-century reliquary with Rhine school enamels on copper, found on the sarcophagus of St. Richard who died during a pilgrimage to Lucca, censers, various types of vestments, miniated books, chalices, a Medieval bronze Arab hawk which was once placed on the pinnacle of the façade, etc.

Going out of the church, behind the apse, you will be able to admire the beautiful bell-tower, which is near the cloisters of San Frediano Monastery, which then became the Royal College.

If you like, you can go up the buttress of the walls. From there you will have the opportunity to see the Apuan Alps.

Church of San Frediano. Chapel Sant'Agostino painted by Amico Aspertini (16th c.). 1. Nativity; 2. Saint Frediano's miracle. Saint Frediano dykes the river Serchio. The miracle is interpreted realistically: in the foreground workers are planting piles on the riverbank, on the nearby hill others are cutting down trees, in the middle the Saint holding a rake makes way for the water, and on the left, portraits of gentlemen among which the assumed self portrait of the painter; 3. Detail of the Nativity; 4. Transportation of the Volto Santo from Luni to Lucca. The Volto Santo is on the cart drawn by heifers in front of which are the clergy and a group of singers. In the background, the port of Luni.

1. Apse and campanile of the Basilica of San Frediano; 2. Partial view of Piazza San Michele; 3. Aerial view of San Frediano.

PIAZZA SAN MICHELE

It is located in a lovely square, in the area of the old Roman square, which has always been the centre of the town. The square was paved again in the 18th century and subdivided by means of small columns and chains. In the 19th century it was adorned with a monument to Francesco Burlamacchi by Ulisse Cambi. Before entering the church we suggest you admire the wrought-iron lights of the beginning of the 16th century, and the **Palazzo Pretorio**, built at the end of the 15th century with a lovely loggia completed in

two phases: in 1492 on a plan by Matteo Civitali or, according to other historians, by his son, Nicolao, and in 1589 by Vincenzo Civitali.

Another interesting building is the **Palazzo del Decanato**, linked to the transept of the church by means of a sort of bridge, attributed to Francesco Marti who built it on the preexisting Palazzo degli Anziani. On one side of the square there are remarkable houses of the 13th and 14th centuries and Palazzo Baldassarre.

The church itself is also called **San Michele ad**

2

Foro or in Foro because of its location. It was built in various successive phases, with very few remaining elements of the original building and clearly showing the following restorations. The lower part of the façade is Romanesque, the upper part is Gothic. The bell-tower was started in the 12th century, but completed only in the 19th century. The church is made of white limestone and has a very high façade surmounted by a Romanesque statue of St. Michael. The decoration is quite impressive, with wonderful small columns which were radically restored in the 19th century (some of them were replaced and taken to the National Museum in Villa Guinigi) and which are surmounted in the second row by the portraits of famous men of that period, such as Garibaldi and King Vittorio Emanuele and so on. Along the two sides there are blank arches and capitals with remarkable trusses and mouldings.

Inside, the church is Romanesque, with three naves and full of art treasures. On the right you have a beautiful glazed terra-cotta Virgin attributed to Andrea della Robbia; on the wall there is a «Martyrdom of St. Andrew» by Pietro Paolini (Lucca, 1435-1525).

In the transept, at the beginning of the presbytery, there is now a 12th-century Lucca school crucifix which originally hung over the centre of the church. On the right, you can admire a panel depicting some Saints by Filippino Lippi and a high-relief of the Virgin with Child which is thought to be a fragment of a 1522 sepulchral monument by Raffaello da Montelupo.

Unfortunately, the old choir which surrounded the central nave was lost. Part of it can be seen in the Museum in Villa Guinigi. The 18th-century High Altar is by Vambrè. The crypt disappeared, probably during one of the many restorations.

3

1. Church of S. Michele (12th c.); 2. Interior; 3. Virgin and Infant. Low relief in glazed terracotta attributed to Andrea della Robbia.

67

Church of San Michele in Foro. Transept, tempera representing the following Saints: Rocco, Sebastian, Jerome, Helen, by Filippino Lippi.

◀ *Church of San Michele in Foro. Crucifix painted on wood by the school of Lucca XIIth century.*

2

3

4

ST. SALVATORE'S CHURCH

Once you are back in Via Santa Giustina, you can go on up to Piazza del Salvatore or della Misericordia, where you can visit a neoclassical *fountain* built in 1842 and the 12th-century *Veglio Tower*, the top of which no longer exists. Then you can move on to the church. Its upper part is in false Gothic (actually built in the 19th century), but the whole building dates back to before 1180. In the right door there is an interesting architrave with the legend of the golden schyphos. The inner naves contain, on the right, in the head, an «Ascension» by Zacchia da Vezzano and the 15th-century Stagi altar, and, on the left, the «Virgin with Saints» by Ardenti.

For those who love music, it might be interesting to have a look at two famous palaces where two renowned musicians were born: **Boccherini** and **Catalani**. The first one is placed in Via Buia, which today is named after Boccherini, whereas the house of the modern singer of Wally is located in Via degli Asili.

1. Piazza San Salvatore with the 12th century church and the neoclassical fountain by Luigi Comolli; 2. Lintel of the righthand side lateral door by Biduino (13th c.); 3. Ruins of the Tower del Veglio; 4. Sant'Agostino's campanile (14th c.). At the foot of the campanile, the ruins of the Roman Theatre.

70

SANTA MARIA CORTEORLANDINI O NERA

Being now in Via Galli Tassi, the next visit will be devoted to **Santa Maria Corteorlandini, or** Santa Maria **Nera**, with an adjacent chapel reproducing the Holy House in Loreto.

The church is named after the ancient Court of Roland, and was built in the 12th century, even though it was internally reconstructed in the 17th century. The Virgin venerated here is a copy of the Virgin in Loreto. The church contains frescoes by Scorzini, paintings by Rosselli, Chiari, Vanni and copies of Guido Reni and Luca Giordano. In the adjacent chapel, named after the Holy House in Loreto, there is a 15th-century wooden statue portraying St. Nicholas from Tolentino, attributed to Cozzarelli. The attached 17th-century convent hosts the State Library with more than half a million precious books, including some miniated codices.

1. Church of Santa Maria Corteorlandini (S. Maria Nera) (12-17th c.); 2. Lateral portal (12th c.); 3. Interior (1719).

71

PALAZZO PFANNER

Going from Via Fillungo to Piazza Sant'Agostino passing through Via San Giorgio, you will be able to admire two very special works of art. The **St. Augustine's bell-tower** has at its base the remains of the ancient Roman theatre (the curved shape of the houses in this area show that they were built on its ruins) which was probably built in the 2nd century. The second masterpiece is the wonderful **Palazzo Pfanner**, formerly called Palazzo Controni, built in the second half of the 17th century on a 16th-century plan. The name of the architect, however, has never been discovered.

The façade is wonderful. The large staircase is supported by pillars and columns and faces a really spectacular garden which is attributed to Juvara. An octagonal pool lies in the centre of the garden and is surrounded by statues representing the four seasons, the twelve months and other subjects. A walk, bordered by high hedges, leads to the lemon-house, surrounded by a balustrade with two lions and one eagle. The trees along the walls are really impressive, and the green spots give a final touch to the whole landscape.

The floor of the palace is made of ancient cotto. Many precious works of art can be founds inside. In

Palazzo Pfanner. Suggestive view of the palace, of the 18th century garden in the middle of which you can see an octogonal basin and the overlooking loggias.

the hall there is a 3rd-century Roman sarcophagus. The first floor was decorated by Scorzini at the beginning of the 18th century. Here you can visit the exhibition of Lucca traditional costumes which are now owned by the Municipality. It is really an interesting collection of piece, either bought or received through donations, including the jacket of the Gonfalonier, otherwise called «delle sessanta minestre», because at those times the Gonfalonier remained in office only fox sixty days.

1

4

2

3

Palazzo Pfanner. Permanent exhibition of Luccan costumes of the 18th, 19th and 20th c. 1. Entrance hall of the palace in a painting by A. Morelli dating back to 1875; 2. Costumes' exhibition room; 3. Man's clothing of various types. Noteworthy is the jacket of the Gonfaloniere della Repubblica di Lucca known as the «sixty soups» and made of red silk gros grain; 4. Man's costume made up of jacket and cloak in red velvet with silver palmshaped embroidery (19th c.).

74

PALAZZO ORSETTI

The wonderful portals by Nicolao Civitali, in carved grey stone have images of sphinxes, dragons, etc., surmounted by a Triton and a Mermaid. The first floor contains valuable furniture and paintings. The staircases are really wonderful.

1. Palazzo Orsetti (16th c.), seat of the Communal Administration; 2. One of the two portals to be found on the two façades. Cornice engraved with coats of arms and grotesques of a magnificent decorating effect; 3. The Green Room of the Palace.

1

2

3

4

Palazzo Orsetti. 1. Red Room; 2. Echo Room; 3. Mirrors' Room; 4. Portrait of Giacomo Puccini by Luigi de Servi executed in 1902.

77

2

PALAZZO MANSI
NATIONAL GALLERY

In Via Galli Tassi you can find the 17th-century **Palazzo Mansi**, which hosts the National Gallery and all its art treasures.

The rooms on the ground floor are devoted to public activities. A marvellous staircase leads to the first floor where you can admire the magnificent rooms with 17th- and 18th-century furniture, Brussels tapestry and the wonderful «Nuptial Room», framed by a baroque golden arch which separate it from the rest of the hall. Embellished as it is with silks, stuccoes and wooden carvings, its beauty, richness and state of preservation are unique.

The rooms nearby contain paintings of great artists of the past: Tintoretto, Veronese, Domenichino, Guido Reni, Palma il Giovane, Calvaert. Most of the collection was donated by the Grand Duke of Tuscany Leopold II, who in 1847 wanted to award the town which had just been annexed to his state, thus compensating the losses suffered by Charles Louis Bourbon.

Palazzo Mansi, seat of the Pinacoteca Nazionale. 1. Brussels tapestries realized after a drawing by Justus Egmont (1665); 2. Portrait of Alessandro de' Medici by Jacopo Carrucci known as il Pontorno; 3. Scipio's abstinence (16th c.) by the Sienese Domenico Beccafumi; 4. Crucifix figuring Saint Catherine of Alexandria and Saint Julius by Guido Reni (17th c.); 5. Portrait of Giacomo Puccini by Edoardo Gelli. On pages 80-81: the magnificent spouses' bedchamber (18th c.).

3

4   5

ST. PAOLINO'S CHURCH

Its construction started in the first part of the 16th century, on a project by Baccio da Montelupo, and it was dedicated to the first bishop of Lucca. It is Latin-cross shaped (though the lateral naves are not very long). It hosts several paintings and wooden sculptures, together with frescoes illustrating the legend of St. Paolino by Certosino (above) and Filippo Gherardi, a 17th-century artist. The first altar on the right, by Riccio, is dedicated to the Holy Trinity; in the second one there is a Virgin with Child and Saints by Ardenti; the third one was made of wood in the 15th century by Francesco Valdambrino; the fourth one, by Testa, tells the story of the miracle of St. Theodore. Beyond the transept there is a 14th wooden crucifix and by its side there is a «Burial of St. Paolino» by Paolo di Lazzarino da Lucca. Another valuable 14th-century wooden work is the Angel placed in a niche. The High Altar dates back to the 16th century. Behind it you can admire an early-Christian sarcophagus. In a niche on the left there is a Certosino wooden sculpture portraying St. Paolino; in the chapel on the left you have the «Coronation of the Virgin» and, in front, a «Virgin with Child and Saints», of the 15th and 16th centuries, respectively. The first altar is adorned with a «Beheading of Valerio» by Guidotti, and the second one with a German terra-cotta depicting the Virgin with Child. The «Pietà» by Lombardi on the fourth altar and some works by Zacchia in the Sacristy are also worth seeing.

1. Church of San Paolino (first half of the 16th c.); 2. Right hand side with view of the campanile; 3. Maria's Coronation between angels and saints, below a view of Lucca in the Middle Ages; Florentine school of the second half of the 15th c.

THE OUTSKIRTS
THE VILLAS

It is almost impossible to recall all the beautiful villas surrounding Lucca. According to someone, there are six-hundred of them. If you have time, it is worthwhile seeing at least the most important ones, if and when they are open to the public, since most of them — except the severely damaged ones — are still inhabited.

The most famous one, the **Marlia Royal Villa**, is also one of the oldest, even though its external appearance dates back to the last century, in the period of Elisa Bonaparte. At the beginning of the 19th century, in its place, there still was the ancient villa of the Count Orsetti, with a wonderful garden and close to the bishop's residence where Lucca's bishops spent their holidays. The present villa is the result of the fusion of these two palaces, and therefore consists of two separate bodies surrounded by a large park and a circle of walls. Let us have a look at its history.

While the bishop's residence was built in the 16th century (today it is practically devoid of what it contained: pieces of furniture, paintings and so on), Palazzo Orsetti was built one century later and partly modified by Elisa Bonaparte. The big fountain facing the palace, the «Palazzina dell'Orologio» (Clock Tower), the statues of the garden, the decorative fountains, all date back to the same period. Other curiosities are the «Teatro di Verdura», the pool with the water theatre and the small lake bordered by beautiful trees.

1. Piazzale in front of Villa Reale, meeting point for guided tours; 2. Tree-lined avenue leading to the entrance of the villa.

VILLA TORRIGIANI

Another spectacular palace is **Torrigiani di Camigliano**, built in the 16th century too, and enlarged and modified by its owner one century later, when it acquired its present name.

Alfonso Torrigiani left the back façade unchanged, but wanted to reconstruct the main one. The result is really sumptuous: statues, balconies, niches and loggias adorn the façade which is remarkable also for the peculiar mixture of materials it was built with: tuff, sandstone, marble, etc.

The entrance portal is magnificent. It faces a garden adorned with pools bordered by long green curtains of high-stem trees. There is a round fountain on the other side too, where a long cypress-bordered promenade begins.

You cannot miss the ornamental waterworks of the Nymphaeum, the small chapel and the artificial medieval «borgo», which is not too far away. The villa is full of precious pieces of furniture and paintings.

Villa Torrigiani is worth a visit, should it be for its beautiful, richly decorated façade, or for its surrounding park and gardens. The two pages illustrate with ample details this marvel.

VILLA MANSI

In **Segromigno** there is another 16th-century **Villa Mansi** which can be visited only in the first floor. An 18th-century architect, Juvara, was responsible for the modifications which embellished the façade and enriched the wonderful garden, full of statues, pools, cascades. The façade was enlarged by Muzio Oddi in the middle of the 17th century. Inside, you can admire Tofanelli's frescoes, Venetian and Lucca pieces of furniture, paintings by Longhi, Pompeo Batoni, Salvator Rosa, Bernardo Bellotto, and a collection of small bronze sculptures of the 16th and 17th centuries. The Clock Tower in the garden was built at the end of the 18th century.

Views of the Villa and of the 18th c. garden of Diana.

1

THE BEAUTIES OF THE PROVINCE

Here you have some proposals to enjoy the province of Lucca, following a rational itinerary and trying not to miss anything really worth seeing.

1) Lucca - Camporgiano, *passing through* **Aquilea, Diecimo, Catureglio, Borgo a Mozzano, Ghivizzano, Coreglia Antelminelli, Barga, Castelvecchio Pascoli, Gallicano, Castelnuovo, Garfagnana, Fornovolasco, Filicaia** *and* **Poggio**.

2) Lucca - Popiglio, *along State Road nr. 12, Abetone, passing through* **San Pietro a Vico, San Cassiano a Vico, Ponte a Moriano, San Giorgio di Brancoli, Ponte a Serraglio, Bagni di Lucca, Bagni Caldi, Benabbio** *and* **San Cassiano.**

3) Lucca - Massarosa, *passing through* **Nozzano, Arliano, Massaciuccoli Lake, Torre del Lago** *and* **Val di Castello.**

4) Lucca - Forte dei Marmi *passing through* **Viareggio, Lido di Camaiore, Marina di Pietrasanta** *and* **Pietrasanta.**

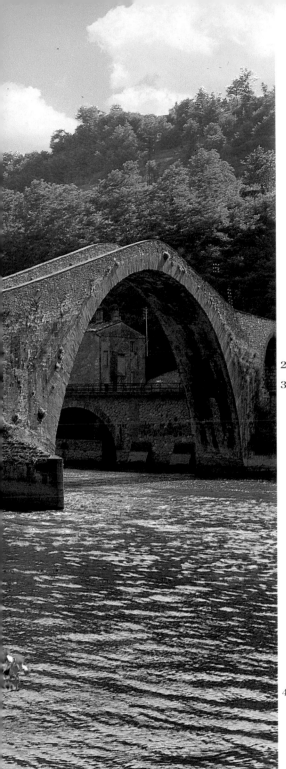

1. Borgo a Mozzano. Ponte del Diavolo (Devil's bridge); 2. Coreglia Antelminelli: panorama; 3-4. Museum of gypsum figurines: the Crib, Cupid and Psyche by Canova and the Apollo di Belvedere by Leocare.

89

1   2

BARGA

Now you can head for **Barga** entering through the *Royal Gate*, with an arch decorated by a terra-cotta Virgin with Child and Angels by Della Robbia. Many interesting buildings are located within the municipality which has also a modern and industrialized area. For instance, the Clare convent, known as *St. Elizabeth Conservatory* with a 15th century church. It hosts an altar piece by Della Robbia, a wooden Crucifix by Della Robbia, etc. Then, there is the church of the *Crocefisso dei Bianchi*, with interesting works inside and from

which you can go up to a wonderful «Observatory», where a marvellous view can be taken. Part of the *Dome* was built as back as the 9th century. It contains 14th-century frescoes, sculptures by Bigarelli's school, terra-cottas by Della Robbia, wooden statues etc. The façade is decorated by a double row of small arches. Close to it there is a tower with merlons serving also as bell-tower. Near the Dome, there is also the *Palazzo Pretorio*.

3

Barga. 1. The cathedral with the Pania in the background; 2. Porta Reale at the entrance of the village; 3. Panorama embracing the castle.

90

Barga. 1. Polychrome wooden statue representing Saint Cristopher supposedly carved around the year 1000; 2. The cathedral; 3. Lintel of the lateral door: low relief representing a convivial scene by Biduino (12th c.); 4. Detail of the pulpit: Nativity and Annunciation.

91

CASTELVECCHIO PASCOLI

We then suggest to go to **Castelvecchio Pascoli**, with the *house* where the poet spent the last years of his life and the chapel where he rests together with his sister Maria. Here Pascoli wrote the «Canti di Castelvecchio» and many other poems.

6

7

8

9

Castelvecchio Pascoli. 1. House of the Poet; 2. Belvedere 3. Detail of the studio; 4. The kitchen; 5. Parish of San Niccolò; 6. Portrait of Giovanni Pascoli (Bruno Cordati); 7-8. Views of Castelnuovo di Garfagnana: the castle; 9. The dried out basin of Bagli and the ruins of the old town.

93

1

4

2

3

5

6

1. The Hermitage of Colomini; 2-3. Views of the Apuan Alps: the Pania della Croce (1858 m) and the Monteforato (1223 m); 4. The Romanesque parish of Brancoli; 5. Grotta del Vento (cave): rising in the background; 6. Grotta del Vento: polychromatic slides; 7-8-9-10. Views of the domanial park of the Orecchiella (1250 m) in Garfagnana, near Castelnuovo; 11. Grotta del Vento: polychromatic ridges; the Grotta del Vento of Fornovolasco is amongst the most interesting natural caves in Europe from a scientifical point of view. It is open to the public and to touristic tours.

95

1

BAGNI DI LUCCA

These hot springs (the water temperature is of 39° to 54° C.) were already known in the Middle ages with the name of Bagni di Corsena. The springs are exploited in all the area. Bagni di Lucca, however, experienced its maximum splendour at the times of Napoleon and the Bourbons, when people from all over Europe used to come here.

Among these illustrious visitors there were Lord Byron, Heine, Montaigne, Shelley, Elizabeth and Robert Browning, and the Italian poets d'Azeglio and Carduc-ci. Here, in 1836, two Frenchmen, Mathis and Ginnestet, built the first *Casino* in Europe. However, since they were not granted the renewal of the concession by the Grand Duke Leopold of Tuscany, they left this area and moved to Monte Carlo, where they founded that famous Casino.

Ponte a Serraglio too, whose construction was encouraged by Castruccio Castracani in the 14th century, is worth being visited. From here you can go up to **Bagni Caldi**, where the thermal baths are located.

From Bagni di Lucca you can also go to Benabbio, whose 13th-century *church*, dedicated to the Assumption, contains a baptysmal font, a 15th-century triptych and two wooden statues by Pietro d'Angelo di Guarnieri, Jacopo della Quercia's father. The ruins of an old castle dominate the village.

2

1. Panoramic view of Bagni di Lucca; 2. Municipal Casino; 3. Botri gorge; 4. Ponte a Serraglio; 5. Panorama of Montefegatesi; 6. Cocciglia ravine; 7. House on the river Lima.

3

4

5

6

7

CASA PUCCINI

You will now move on to the **Massaciuccoli lake** where there are the ruins of the ancient Nero's thermal baths (2nd century) and of a Roman villa. From here you can reach **Torre del Lago**, not so much for its artistic value, since it is a modern town, but to visit the **House of Giacomo Puccini**, who composed most of his music here linking his name to that of the town.

The visit to the house, open to the public, will be particularly interesting. Inside, there still are pieces of furniture and other objects of the composer who rests in the chapel built in one of the rooms.

6

5

1. Lake Massaciuccoli (in the background the Migliarino scrub and the Tyrrhenian Sea); 2. View of Torre del Lago; 3. Villamuseum of Giacomo Puccini; 4. Lyrical season at Torre del Lago: a scene from «La Tosca»; 5. Viale dei Tigli (Linden Lane) leading from Torre del Lago to Viareggio; 6. Giacomo Puccini.

99

INDEX

The photographs are by:
Ascanio Ascani - Misano (Forlì)
Chilardi - Lucca / Maurizio Corti - Lucca
Carlo Fogliati - Lucca / Federico Frassinetti - Bologna
Leonello Mazzotti / Renzo Santori - Lucca
The photographs on page 74 are owned by the Commune of Lucca
The photographs 5 and 6 and II on pp. 94-95 are by Vittorio Verole - Bo
and represent the Grotta del Vento of Fornovolasco

Graphics and typesetting:
FEDERICO FRASSINETTI

Translation: Art - Bologna

editions ITALCARDS
bologna - italy

Updated edition
Printed at the
Fotometalgrafica Emiliana printing press.
S. Lazzaro di Savena (Bologna)